GW00469783

Love Univer
How to survive and thrive at university

ISBN: 9781704441382

2023 edition

Ned Browne

Love University © Ned Browne 2023

Although every care has been taken in writing this publication and ensuring the information contained in it is correct, Ned Browne cannot accept any responsibility for errors or omissions, or for the consequences of any reliance on the information provided.

Note: All facts, figures and URLs are correct at time of writing.

First published in Great Britain 2020.

This edition (third edition) was first published in 2023.

By the same author:

How to get onto the property ladder *- A first-time buyer's guide to financing and finding your first home*

The A-Z of Amazon.co.uk FBA *- A step-by-step guide to branding, sourcing and selling private-label FBA products on Amazon's UK website*

Contents

Introduction

Most young people thrive at university. But many do not - some drop out and others leave with a sense of dissatisfaction. Higher fees are definitely, at least in part, to blame. When you're paying a lot of money, you expect an awesome experience. But the reality is this: the more you put in, the more you'll get out. It's up to you to make sure your university years are the best years of your life.

Before you go to university

The summer holiday before university will be a well-earned break. Most students will have just completed their A levels, which means that 13 years of school / college are behind you. So, enjoy your downtime. Some things you may want to consider doing:

- Go on holiday with your school/college/home friends.
- Get a job and save some money.
- Arrange a leaving party.
- Prepare for your course.
- Open a student bank account (more on student bank accounts later).
- Learn how to cook a few simple meals.
- Learn how to operate a washing machine.
- Read everything your university sends you. There may be important tasks for you to complete before you are fully enrolled. It is, for example, reasonably common for students to lose their place in a hall of residence because they did not complete the required paperwork in time.
- Join Facebook freshers' groups, run by Students' Union officers. There will be loads of useful posts: important deadlines, events, move-in days etc. Social media and online forums are also useful tools to meet people on your courses or in your halls. Facebook, TikTok, Twitter and Instagram are all worth checking out - the website algorithms will serve up useful suggestions too.

What to bring to university

Listed below are some generic things you should consider bringing. Obviously, some of these will be superfluous if you're going to live somewhere with a fully-equipped kitchen:

- Duvet, duvet cover, pillows, pillowcases and sheets.
- Sleeping bag.

- Towels.
- Can opener.
- Scissors.
- Swiss army knife.
- Extension power cable.
- Stationery.
- Plates, cutlery, mugs, pots and pans.
- Peeler, cheese grater and tea towels.
- Tupperware boxes.
- Chargers for all your electronic devices.
- Lots of clothes.
- Earplugs.
- Washbag.
- First Aid kit.
- Toiletries and cosmetics.
- Hairdryer.
- Bank cards.
- Printed copies of your updated CV.
- National Insurance number.
- Driving licence.
- Passport (and/or other forms of photo ID).
- University correspondence (e.g. acceptance letter, accommodation contract and student finance documents).

Student accommodation

More and more students are choosing to live at home, which is a massive shame. If you want to get the most out of university, you need to flee the nest. University isn't just about getting a degree, it's about acquiring life skills - and you can't do that while your parents cook and clean for you. Plus, lots of students who choose to live at home find the time and cost of commuting to university erodes the money they've saved on accommodation. It's worth noting that research has revealed that most students choose to live at home due to financial constraints. So, carefully consider where you study - student.com publishes an annual "Global Student Accommodation Indicator" which shows the huge differences in accommodation costs across the United Kingdom. London was, unsurprisingly, the most expensive city, whereas Hull was the cheapest.

How to find somewhere to live. The sooner you start looking for accommodation, the better. Needless to say, this is easier if you definitely know where you want to study (and you're confident that you'll get the required grades). If this is you, "early" means no later than June.
Assuming you didn't select "living at home" on your UCAS application, each university that's made you an offer should send you a link detailing what accommodation is available. If you don't have this, Google "university name + accommodation". If you did select "living at home" on your UCAS application and you've now changed your mind, contact your chosen university - this should be an easy change to make.

Where to live. For most students there are two choices: live in halls of residence or rent privately from a landlord. University halls of residence are provided by and managed by the university. There are privately owned halls too. Most halls of residence house tens or hundreds of students (often in the same year group). Some universities offer halls of residence for all students in every year group. Most guarantee halls for first-year students. Private rented accommodation is offered by private landlords and mainly comprises properties that accommodate from three to eight students. There are pros and cons to each.

Halls of residence - Pros
- Halls are a great way to meet new people - and that's especially important in your first year.
- Halls provide a stepping stone to the real world. You won't, for example, have to worry about utility bills and wifi.
- Some halls are catered. In other words, there will be a dining hall and set meal times. Don't expect gourmet food, but it should be a step up from school food.
- Almost all halls employ cleaners, so that's one less thing to worry about.

Halls of residence - Cons
- Halls are often more expensive than private rented accommodation. It's easy to be lured in by the offer of ensuite bathrooms and other luxuries, but you will pay for these.
- You have to pay a deposit, which you will only get back if the university is satisfied that you have not caused any damage beyond expected wear and tear. The student body may be considered collectively responsible for any damage, so that means you could end up with a reduced deposit as a result of the acts of others.
- Lack of independence. You will have more rules to follow if you live in halls.

Note: In private halls you are more likely to end up living with students from different universities (especially in cities and towns with more than one university). There are luxury private halls too - so if money isn't an issue Google "luxury student accommodation" to find out what's on offer.

Top tip: Find out exactly what's included in your hall fees. What's on offer will vary widely. For example, some fees include all meals; others will include none.

Top tip: Many students make their first friendships in halls of residence. And that's definitely easier if there are great communal spaces. Your room is where you sleep and, really, isn't that important - it's better to have awesome communal spaces.

Top tip: Write down in your calendar the date your first choice university allows you to start booking accommodation. And take action on that date - the best halls get booked up fast. Otherwise you may end up with accommodation that's more expensive than expected, further from university etc.

Private renting - Pros
- Private renting tends to be cheaper, especially in larger house shares.
- It's great preparation for life - you will need to cook, clean, manage the bills etc.
- You get to choose your housemates.

Private renting - Cons
- You will be responsible for paying all the bills: gas, electricity, water, council tax, TV licence, wifi etc.
- You will be responsible for cleaning the property.
- Most landlords are very reasonable, but some landlords are hideous. There are stories of tenants

being scammed out of their deposits and landlords refusing to repair things that break.
- You have to pay a deposit, which you will only get back if your landlord is satisfied that you have not caused any damage beyond expected wear and tear. Note: By law your landlord is legally required to put your deposit in a government-backed tenancy deposit scheme. There's no harm in asking if this has happened.

How to find the best properties
Start your search early - as that's when the best properties will still be available. Everyone will have their own list of wants, but being reasonably close to your lectures, being reasonably priced and being in a good state of repair would be on most people's wish list. There are other important factors:
- Some residential areas will not welcome students, especially those with an active social life.
- If you like BBQs, you're going to need a garden.

Note: In September 2022 there was a critical shortage of student accommodation in many areas across the UK. Tax changes and interest rate rises have pushed many landlords to sell their properties. For example, between November 2019 and November 2022, the number of rental properties available in London dropped by 20%. This has driven rents up and renters have had to scramble to secure properties. Moreover, many universities have been slow to build more student accommodation to counter this shortfall. So, to reiterate what I said earlier, you will need to be speedy if you want to secure good accommodation.

Top tips for finding private rented accommodation

- All universities will have a student accommodation team offering help and advice on finding a suitable place to live. Most will know about rogue landlords and will have lists of available accommodation. These guys are your first port of call.
- Private student accommodation could be anything from a bedsit to a ten-bedroom mansion. It's horses for courses; choose the one that's best for you.
- If you're viewing a prospective property, try to speak to the current tenants. They will give you a far more honest property appraisal than the letting agents.
- Don't be rushed when viewing properties. Here are some things to check for:
    - Is there enough storage space?
    - Is there room to store your bike?
    - Is there mould in the bathroom (or anywhere else)?
    - Are there locks on the downstairs windows?
    - Is there condensation on the windows?
    - Do the kitchen appliances look in good working order?
    - What does the Energy Performance Certificate (EPC) look like? E-rated properties will cost a LOT more to heat than A-rated properties. And they will be horribly cold during the winter months. Note: From 2025 all new tenancies must have an EPC of no lower than C-rated, which should help reduce bills.
    - Does the landlord have various safety documents that are legally required (such as the Gas Safety Certificate)?

- There are also rogue landlord databases available online. But, at the time of writing, although they are getting better, they're still not very good. Google to find out more information about what's out there near your university of choice.

Important: Never sign a contract unless you are sure you will be able to afford to pay the rent. Take a hard look at your budget - you don't want your rent to gobble up too much money. If you're set on accommodation that will stretch your budget, try to land a part-time job as soon as possible.

How to choose the best housemates

If you choose to rent privately in your first year, this might be potluck. Hopefully, you will end up living with people you like. However, if you're moving from halls of residence to private rented accommodation (as many students do in their second or third years), you need to choose wisely. Here are the golden rules:
- Avoid house shares with couples (and avoid sharing with your partner). If the relationship ends, it could cause misery for everyone in the property. Plus it can be very painful for the ex-couple.
- Choose positive people who are likely to help you become the best version of yourself. Negative people are so draining.
- Think about how much time you will spend with your housemates. If you're on the same course, play for the same teams, have joined the same clubs etc., you might find that's too much time together. Sometimes it's better to live with people with different interests.

- Party people. Choose people with a similar lifestyle. If you're a party person, choose to live with party people. If you're a lark, choose to live with early risers. If you're a vegan, choose to live with vegans.
- Tidiness. If you're a very tidy person, having messy flatmates will start to grate after a while. Try to choose people who are like-minded.

Top tip: Many students find it hard to get their deposit back. Sometimes, this is reasonable, as damage has been caused. Sometimes, it isn't. Here are some ways you can protect yourself:
- Take lots of photos when you first move in (e.g. of the walls, the carpets, the bathroom and the oven). This can be used as evidence if a dispute arises.
- Completely empty and thoroughly clean the property when you move out.
- If a check-out inspection has been arranged, make sure you or one of the other tenants attends.

If you're renting privately, your landlord must return your deposit within 10 days of you both agreeing how much money you will get back. Should a dispute arise with your landlord, then your deposit will be protected in the tenancy deposit scheme until the issue is resolved. Each tenancy deposit scheme has a resolution service.
But, tell your landlord you plan to use the service, as they may then try to resolve the situation before the formal process goes ahead.

Top tip: Always read the small print. You will need to sign a contract (which will be co-signed by your landlord) - this is known as a tenancy agreement, and it sets out the legal terms and conditions of the tenancy. The most common form of tenancy agreement is an Assured Shorthold Tenancy (AST). With this contract, in theory, your landlord can evict you without a reason. In reality, this is unlikely, as you'll only be living there for a year or two. The important thing is this: make sure you have a break clause in the contract. If you have a break clause, you can end the tenancy early provided you give the landlord enough warning. During the Covid pandemic, many students had to carry on paying rent even though universities had shut and they were no longer living in the property. A break clause would have prevented this. Also, don't sign up for a full year, if you only need accommodation from, for example, September to July.

Front door locks. When you move in, ask your landlord to change the front-door locks, especially if the property has been tenanted before. Also, if there isn't a chain on the door, ask your landlord to fit one.

Your room. Make your room your oasis. Student accommodation can be messy, loud, cluttered and crowded. It's important to have a sanctuary. Adding a few personal touches to your room will make it feel more homely too.

Living at home. If you decide (or are compelled) to live at home, it will be harder to reap the full benefits of university. Here are some things you should consider:
- Do not yo-yo from home to university just attending lectures and tutorials. University is far more than your academic studies.
- Join at least two clubs and/or societies – and go every week, rain or shine. Even if you don't feel you fit in initially, you will gradually make friends.
- Form study groups with students on your course, and meet regularly in the library.

- Go to social events, especially those taking place at the Students' Union. Also, consider trying to get a job at the Students' Union.
- Don't rely on social media to keep in touch with people you meet. You cannot beat spending time with people IRL.
- If your parents insist on still treating you like a child, have calm, courageous conversations. Explain that it's only through experience that you'll gain the skills and knowledge you need to survive in the real world.
- Consider moving out, even if it's just for your last year.

Student finance

This section is mainly aimed at students in England, Wales and Northern Ireland. If you're fortunate enough to live in Scotland and decide to study at a Scottish university, university is effectively free. But, for students who live in England, Wales and Northern Ireland things are less rosy.

Tuition fees were introduced by the Labour Government in autumn 1998. At the time, they were just £1,000 a year. However, since then they have been tripled twice: once in 2006 (to £3,000) and again in 2012 (to £9,000). At the time of writing, the current cap is £9,250 per annum. And, although it's a cap, almost all universities charge the maximum amount. Of course, there are maintenance loans too, which are up to a maximum of £12,382 (if you're living away from home and studying in London). These figures change every year, so check for up-to-date information. Please note: You pay your tuition fees with your tuition fee loan - and this is paid directly from the Student Loans Company to your university (i.e. you never see this money). Your maintenance loan is paid in three instalments over the course of the academic year. Provided you applied in plenty of time, you should be paid in September, January and April.

The tripling of tuition fees to £9,000 in 2012 at first glance looks utterly galling. However, the government did sugar the pill: they raised the repayment income threshold to £27,295. But, the government then removed the sugar: for students starting their degree in September 2023, this is being reduced to £25,000. Repayments are then calculated at 9% of your gross salary above that amount. If you don't pay it all off in 40 years, the remaining debt is written off. (Note: The remaining debt was previously written off after 30 years - another change negatively affecting students starting their degree in 2023.)

However, instead of thinking of student loans as debt, it might be better to think of them as a tax on success. If you earn a lot of money, you may well end up paying off all of your loan. However, if this is the case, the amount you earn will almost certainly be, at least in part, due to your education. But, in reality, most people will never fully repay their student loans - recent research suggested that 80% of people will fall into this camp.

Here's a worked example, for any student starting university from September 2023 onwards:

Salary	Amount of salary from which 9% will be deducted	Monthly repayment
£30,000.00	£5,000	£37.50
£35,000.00	£10,000	£75.00
£40,000.00	£15,000	£112.50
£45,000.00	£20,000	£150.00
£50,000.00	£25,000	£187.50
£55,000.00	£30,000	£225.00
£60,000.00	£35,000	£262.50

So, whilst student loans are not good, don't be misled by the mainstream press: they are not an albatross around your neck, and should NEVER put anyone off studying at university. If there are other reasons to discount university as an option, that's fine. But, please don't let it be money.

In addition, it should be noted that, according to the Department for Education, the median graduate salary is approximately £10,000 more than the median non-graduate salary. Over the course of your working life, that's a lot of extra cash. And, for female graduates, that figure is higher.

How much you can borrow
Tuition fee loan - All students can borrow the full amount of their tuition fees, which is almost always £9,250 per academic year. This is paid directly from the Student Loans Company to the university.
Maintenance loan - This money is used by students to cover their rent and day-to-day living costs. The amount you can borrow largely depends on two factors: your household income and where you are living. If, for example, you come from a low-income household and are living away from home in London, you are likely to receive the highest amount. Conversely, if your parents are high earners and you're living at home, expect far less money. There's an online calculator which you can use to work out how much you will be likely to get:
https://www.gov.uk/student-finance-calculator

Note: Perversely, there have been many cases of students from higher-income households hitting financial problems, as their parents did not appreciate that they are expected to make up the shortfall. If you think that might be you, have that conversation as soon as possible. In fact, show them this paragraph - it could well save you an unpleasant argument!

The table below shows the maximum amount you can borrow as of 2022/2023. Please note: at the time of writing, the government hasn't published the 2023/2024 figures.

	2022 to 2023 academic year
Living with your parents	Up to £8,171
Living away from your parents, outside London	Up to £9,706
Living away from your parents, in London	Up to £12,667

Top Tip: Complete your student finance application soon after making your firm and insurance university choices on UCAS. This will ensure your money arrives in time and that you can iron out any problems with your application.

Interest on student loans
Student-loan debt vs. mortgage debt

The rate of interest is based on the Retail Price Index (RPI) rate of inflation. (There are two measures of inflation: the Retail Price Index (RPI) and the Consumer Price Index (CPI). The only thing you need to know is that the RPI is almost always the higher measure of inflation. This is because, in simple terms, RPI includes housing costs whereas CPI does not.)

The government hasn't published the figures for students starting in 2023, but they are likely to be similar to what's below (but expect the £27,295 to change to £25,000). Here's how it's calculated (based on someone who took out a student loan from 2012 onwards):

- If you earn £27,295 or less, you pay just the RPI rate of inflation.

- If you earn between £27,296 and £49,130, you pay RPI plus an interest rate that will gradually rise from RPI to RPI + 3% the more you earn.
- If you earn over £49,130 you pay the RPI rate of inflation + 3%.

The RPI rate is set every September using the rate from March of the same year.

Note: Due to rising inflation in 2022 the government imposed new rules to help protect graduates from ever-rising student debt - student loan interest rates were capped at 6.3% from September 2022.

Top tip: The Student Loans Company is a dreadful organisation. Don't take my word for this, check out their reviews on Trustpilot - 1% of students rated them as Excellent (the highest rating) as opposed to 96% of students who rated them as Bad (the lowest rating). So, do not expect helpful customer service or a speedy processing of your application.

Bursaries, grants, scholarships etc.
There is a lot of additional funding available for students. However, you need to be prepared to jump through a few hoops to get the cash. You are most likely to be able to access this additional money if:

- You come from a low-income household.
- You are a care leaver.
- You have some sort of disability.
- You are particularly talented in a certain field.

Finding available funding will take time and research. But, if you are successful, it will be time well spent. Here are the main types of funding:

Bursaries. This is money made available by an educational institution (or funding authority) to students. It is normally allocated to students who would not be able to attend university without this money. It's also used to encourage specific groups or individuals to attend university (for example, care leavers or students from low-income households). Bursaries do not have to be repaid.

Grants. Government grants are available to students in Wales and Northern Ireland. Similar to bursaries, they are means-tested. For students in Northern Ireland there is, for example, the Maintenance Grant (nidirect.gov.uk/articles/maintenance-grant). For students in Wales, there's the Welsh Government Learning Grant and Special Support Grant (SSG) - Google either of these names for details or head to Student Finance Wales (studentfinancewales.co.uk). Some businesses, charities and councils also provide grants.

Scholarships. These are available to students who are high achievers. But they are not just for academic high achievers. There are also, for example, musical scholarships, financial need scholarships, personal circumstance scholarships and sporting achievement scholarships.

Sponsored Degrees (AKA Degree Apprenticeships). These are school leaver programmes offered by companies that allow you to graduate debt free (while also gaining valuable work experience). You will be paid a salary too. These programmes are highly competitive, not least because many are offered by some of the country's best employers. There are a few downsides though: you won't have long holidays, a big chunk of your time will be spent at work, and it will take you longer to graduate. To find out more, head to ucas.com and click on Apprenticeships.

Sponsorship. Some companies and organisations fund or part-fund degree students. The trade off being that you will probably be obliged to work for them when you graduate (for a predetermined length of time).

Disabled Students' Allowance (DSA). This is provided to students with a wide range of "disabilities" including such things as dyspraxia and dyslexia. Any DSA funding you receive doesn't have to be repaid and DSA funding isn't means-tested (i.e. even affluent students are eligible for DSA). For more details, click on this link: gov.uk/disabled-students-allowances-dsas Note: The Equality Act 2010 and the United Nations (UN) Convention on the Rights of Persons with Disabilities help to enforce, protect and promote the rights of people with disabilities. It's against the law for universities to treat disabled students unfavourably. Your university also has a duty to make "reasonable adjustments" to ensure disabled students are not discriminated against. These changes could include providing extra support and aids (for example, specialist equipment). All universities will also have a person responsible for disability issues who you can talk to about the support they offer.

Note: There is no substitute for thoroughly researching the different types of funding available to you. This chapter has not been written to give you all the answers (otherwise it would run to a few thousand pages). Instead it has been written to get you thinking and to convince you to take action. You may be surprised by what you find. For example, a grant of up to £500 is available from The Vegetarian Charity, and money is also available for talented eSports players.

Finding scholarships, bursaries, sponsorship and grants

- The best place to head is The Scholarship Hub (thescholarship hub.org.uk). This website is by far the most comprehensive source of information available.
- Your university website. Especially for funding opportunities unique to that university.
- Two other excellent sources of information are Save The Student (savethestudent.org) and MoneySavingExpert (moneysavingexpert.com).

Your first week at university

This can be an overwhelming week, especially if you've moved away from home for the first time. It's a hugely exciting time too though. Remember, most other students will be in the same boat, so you're not really alone. Now is the time to introduce yourself to as many people as possible and explore what your university has to offer.

Different people. Universities are broad churches: expect to meet people from all walks of life - different races, religions, sexualities, countries, regions etc. Universities tend to have very strong LGBTQ+ communities too. This heterogeneity is one of the things that makes university life so enriching. Universities embrace diversity and so should you. Meeting people with different backgrounds and beliefs is a great way to learn new things and to learn to think in different ways. Do not prejudge anyone: often the most unlikely students become the stars of the future.

Freshers' week. This is a festival of events that welcomes new university students. It's also a crucial week: there will be admin tasks you need to get done; there will be people to meet; and there will be clubs and societies to join. The freshers' week normally takes place before formal lectures begin, so you're as free as a bird. Attend as many events as you can – sitting in your room watching Netflix is not an option.

Freshers' fair. This will take place in a hall and will consist of dozens of stalls. Sign up for everything that takes your fancy. Don't hand over any money though. Signing up to a club or society doesn't commit you to attending for the next three years. Instead, attend a few meetings to see whether or not it's for you. Joining a club or society is a great way to make new friends. And having lots of hobbies and interests looks great on your CV too. Also, during freshers' fairs they give out loads of freebies - fill your boots!

Administrative tasks. These will vary from university to university. Below is a list that most students will have to (or should) do:

- **University registration.** This is normally done online before you arrive at university. But, you will have to collect your ID card and you may need to provide requested documentation.
- **Library.** You will probably need to register before you can use the library resources.
- **Doctor/dentist.** Try to register with a local doctor and dentist. Also, find out the address of your nearest A&E department (just in case).
- **Get your bearings.** This might involve finding where your lectures are going to be held, finding your nearest supermarket, working out the quickest/safest route to university or tracking down your closest Post Office.
- **Save the university 24/7 security number on your phone**. This can be helpful during emergencies.

Students' Unions. This should be your first port of call once you've unpacked. Students' Unions are run by student representatives (reps) who have been elected by students. The student reps are, effectively, the voice of the student body. Students' Unions differ from university to university, but broadly they all undertake the following functions:

- Provide students with support, help, advice and guidance.
- Oversee the numerous student societies and clubs.
- Act as a student hub - most will have coffee shops, social areas and bars.
- Organise competitions, exhibitions, gigs or social events.

- Provide students with jobs (such as bar staff jobs).

Nightlife. You've made it to university - that's an awesome achievement. And, yes, you should party and relish the social side of university life (that's pretty hard to beat). So, enjoy every single moment. But stay safe too (see the "Health and wellbeing" section in the book for more details).

Homesickness. If you're feeling homesick (which is defined by the Cambridge Dictionary as "feeling unhappy because of being away from home for a long period"), remember this: no matter how prepared you are to live on your own, how well organised and independent you think you are, it is normal to feel lonely at times during your first few weeks. All students do, as everyone is in a new environment, managing everything by themselves. Plus you no longer have your support network of family and friends to hand. For many students, feelings of homesickness will pass in a matter of weeks. But, short term, seeing your old friends (even via Zoom) will give you a lift. As will forcing yourself out of your room and meeting new people.

However, if you find you can't shake it, please don't suffer in silence. Universities take mental-health issues very seriously and should be able to provide support and guidance. You'll be able to find out how to access their services by looking for Student Welfare on your university's website.

Top tlp: During your first week, write a letter to yourself listing what you want to achieve while you're at university. Yes, this is a bit of a hackneyed idea, but it's still a good one. Alternatively, write down your university "bucket list" and keep it pinned to your wall.

How to be amazing

To be amazing you have to be different. You may have to be single-minded, stubborn, resilient and brave too. This chapter has been written to give you some ideas and, hopefully, to inspire you as well.

Writing. The following authors wrote their first book while at university: Zadie Smith, Bret Easton Ellis and Veronica Roth. But don't be daunted: you don't have to start by writing a book. Why not start a blog instead? If there's something you're passionate about, choose that - if, for example, you love films, blog your film reviews. Also, many universities have their own student newspapers - track them down and ask them to publish your articles. If they say "no" ask again, and keep on asking until they say "yes". And if there isn't a student newspaper... result! Start your own - pretty much every university has funding available for students wanting to start new clubs or societies.

If you have some work you'd like to get published, don't write off self-publishing - it's come a long way in recent years. So, if you've written poetry, a short story or a play, check out Amazon's Kindle Direct Publishing (kdp.amazon.com/en_US). There are other self-publishing platforms, but none have the reach of Amazon.

Entrepreneurship. University is a great time to start a business. You will have the time and support you need to get things up and running. Start small if need be: dog walking, babysitting, selling your art on Etsy, flogging unwanted textbooks on Amazon, tutoring GCSE students or signing up with taskrabbit.co.uk (for all manner of different tasks). But be ambitious too. There is likely to be an entrepreneurs' club - join this (or start your own). There you will meet students with similar ambitions and you'll have a sounding board for your ideas. They should be able to put you in touch with business mentors too. So, whether you want to start your own fashion label or create an app, you'll be able to find people to help. Shell LiveWIRE is also worth checking out - they provide support for young entrepreneurs (www.livewire.shell).

Young entrepreneurs can also get help from the Prince's Trust (princes-trust.org.uk), who offer advice and guidance on everything from marketing to funding your business idea. They can also provide you with a business plan template. Moreover, the Prince's Trust works with the Start Up Loans Company to offer business loans between £500 to £25,000.

If you have an innovative business idea, you may want to consider crowdfunding your idea. On top of raising money, you can also showcase your business idea. Google "crowdfunding UK" for more details.

Top tip: If you think you have a great business idea, beware: loose lips sink ships. Get a non-disclosure agreement (NDA) drawn up - they're available free online. Cameron and Tyler Winklevoss famously shared their social networking idea with Mark Zuckerberg. And, yes, they didn't get him to sign a non-disclosure agreement.

Sport. If you excel at sport, university is a great place to take your skills to another level. Almost all universities have superb sporting facilities and sports clubs. You'll be able to compete in almost any sporting activity you can imagine. If you are keen to focus on one specific sport, seek out the university (or university town) that's a hotbed for that sport, for example, Bath for rugby. And don't limit yourself to university clubs. Seek out the professional and semi-professional teams too.

University is also a great place to take up new sports. Most schools have a very limited range of sporting opportunities; this is not the case at university. Joining sports clubs is also a great way to meet new people and makes staying fit far less of a chore.

Events. A lot of events taking place at universities across the country are organised by the students. Organising events can be stressful and time consuming. But it's also hugely rewarding and will equip you with numerous life skills. Here are some ideas:

- **Comedy night**. Either invite established comedians or have an open mic event (or a combination of the two). It's easier than you think to persuade people in the public eye to sign up. So, get on the phone, Tweet and send those emails. As an aside, pubs often have rarely-used function rooms and many will welcome an event that could help them drum up some business.
- **TEDx talk**. The very first TEDx event, which took place on 23rd March 2009, was a university event. TED is always keen to work with universities. So, if you have an inspiring lecturer or tutor, get them on the stage. TED's website (ted.com) has information that will help guide you through the process.
- **Fashion shows**. At the time of writing, 120 universities offered fashion or fashion-related courses. That's a lot of fashion students! Even if you aren't a fashion student, you can still get involved - it takes a lot of people to organise a fashion show. The same applies for students at universities that don't offer fashion courses. As an aside, the fashion industry in the United Kingdom is massive, employing over half a million people.
- **Live music**. Big name artists tend to avoid university

venues (which are usually the preserve of bands on the way up and bands on the way down). But smaller performers may be easier to pin down. If you want to have some fun, it's hard to beat a "battle of the bands" event.

- **Balls.** Dressing down is one of the joys of university - especially if you've had to endure school uniforms and sixth-form dress codes. Dressing up is fun too though. Lots of clubs and societies will host summer balls. Jump on board - and make yours the best ever. **Top tip:** Book your venue and start selling tickets early. You won't be the only show in town.
- **Meet the alumni coffee morning**. Attending a university is a bit like supporting a football club - you can't change allegiance. Most graduates have fond memories of their university days and many will be happy to support those same universities. Meeting past students is a great way to learn from their experiences and network. Moreover, universities will hold databases of their alumni, and should be happy to help promote your event.
- **Club nights**. Turn down the lights, turn up the volume and put the DJ centre stage. Not all universities have nightclubs on their doorsteps, but all have venues that can be transformed into nightclubs. Again, you'll have the choice of hiring professional DJs or finding student DJs.
- **Art exhibitions**. Universities are hubs of creativity, but sometimes it's a struggle to get your work noticed. Curating an art exhibition will benefit all parties. Make sure you create an online catalogue of the work too - and email the link to artists of note and established galleries.

- **Pop-up shops.** This could be anything from a pop-up coffee shop to a range of stalls selling a variety of goods. If it's the latter, it could be a combination of student stalls, club/society stalls and local businesses.

Top tip: Universities, like all educational institutions, take health and safety very seriously. If you are arranging any event that involves a large group of students, engage with those in charge as early as possible. They will, after all, hold the keys to the venues (figuratively and literally).

Charity. In the beautiful words of Martin Luther King, "Every man must decide whether he will walk in the light of creative altruism or in the darkness of destructive selfishness." Of course, were he alive today, he would have surely said man or woman. Some university students have raised tens of thousands of pounds for charity. So, if there's a cause close to your heart, getting involved in charity work is a great use of your time.

Raising money for good causes. There are countless ways to raise money, from bake sales to sponsored runs, from creating events to egg painting. The Giving Machine website (thegivingmachine.co.uk/fundraising-ideas) has a seemingly never-ending list of ideas.

It is, of course, the digital age. With a limited budget, smart use of social media is the best way to boost the profile of your fundraising (and, therefore, boost the amount of money you raise). Start off by setting up a fundraising page on, for example, justgiving.com and then link all your social media to that.

Micro charity donations. There are lots of ways to give money to charity at little cost to yourself. Amazon and eBay, for example, both run schemes linked to your purchases. You can also donate your Nectar and Tesco Clubcard points to charity.

Campaigning. If there is something you feel strongly about, you can campaign for change. This can be on a local level (for example, campaigning to stop a community facility being closed) or on a national level (for example, campaigning against corporation tax avoidance). Campaigning can help give a voice to those without one, or bring together disparate voices. The tools of campaigners are wide and varied, but mainly involve raising the profile of the issue. To find out about existing campaigns, or to find guidance to help you set up your own campaign, head to: nusconnect.org.uk

Note: According to the human rights charity Liberty, the Government's Police, Crime, Sentencing and Courts Act (the Policing Act), that came into effect in April 2022, will also have a serious impact on human rights, particularly the right to protest. Please make sure you know your rights, especially if you're planning on engaging in direct action, such as blocking oil depots.

Volunteering. Many of the most vulnerable in society rely on volunteers. But finding volunteering opportunities can be surprisingly hard (especially ones that are right for you). A good starting point is researching local charities and contacting them directly Phone and email (just sending an email is far less likely to produce results). Charities don't have large budgets to spend on advertising for volunteers; that's why you'll often see volunteer adverts on the doors of charity shops. Your university should also be able to help you find opportunities.

Finally, the government has a volunteering portal (gov.uk/government/get-involved/take-part/volunteer), which is a bit clunky, but might give you some ideas. Volunteering is also a great way to learn new skills and improve your CV.

Some other ways you can make the world a better place:

- **Giving blood**. The NHS needs a constant supply of blood for a variety of reasons. By volunteering to give blood, you will save lives. To find out how, go to blood.co.uk
- **Stem cell registers**. Stem cells are used to treat a wide range of blood cancers and disorders. For some people, a stem cell transplant is their only hope of survival. But matching donors and patients isn't easy. This is even more difficult if you're in an ethic minority group. For example, 80% of African-Caribbean patients are not currently able to find a matching donor. By signing up as a donor, you may be able to save a life. So, get yourself on the register by contacting one of the many amazing charities supporting this work, such as the ACLT (aclt.org) and Anthony Nolan (anthonynolan.org).
- **Organ donation**. It's never good to think about death. But if, in death, you can save someone else's life, that has to be a good thing. You can register your organ donation preferences here: organdonation.nhs.uk
- **Raising awareness**. This is as important as raising money. So, find a charity that's close to your heart and retweet their tweets, share their YouTube videos, wear their T-shirts and put up their posters.

Making music. Lots of artists, including M.I.A, Queen, Coldplay and Public Enemy, started out at university. So, find out where the musicians hang out, and get involved. Don't worry if you don't play an instrument or can't sing - these are both things you can learn. Or, if that's not your bag, you can write lyrics or promote gigs.

There are backstage opportunities too, from lighting to stage set construction. But more than anything else, enjoy the music and the scene. As an aside, the music industry is another behemoth - and one where relevant hands-on experience is often valued above qualifications.
Getting your music out there has never been easier. Setting up a YouTube channel is pretty straightforward. Also, over 70 UK universities have their own radio station, who should be happy to play original music (especially anything produced by their own students).
It's also never too late to learn how to play a musical instrument. You'll probably be able to blag free lessons from your fellow students or use YouTube tutorials.

Film & theatre. Hollywood film director, Christopher Nolan, wrote and filmed a number of short films while studying at University College London (including the super-weird *Doodlebug*, currently available on YouTube). Obviously, few directors reach the dizzying heights of Nolan, but that's not the point. If you want to write a screenplay, direct a theatre production, make a short film, design a theatre set, learn about special effects etc., you will have the time and equipment you need to make that happen. You will also be surrounded by thousands of other students, many of whom will be willing to help. As an aside, many university theatre groups take their productions to international events, such as The Edinburgh Festival. For many, this will be a once-in-a-lifetime opportunity.

Podcasts/internet radio. The word "podcast" is a portmanteau (a combination of "iPod" and "broadcast"). Podcasting opened up the world of spoken-word broadcasting to the masses; anyone can now record an audio clip and make it available to those with an internet connection. There are now podcasts covering thousands of topics, but there's always room for more.

So, if you think you have something interesting to say/discuss, podcasting might be for you. Start by listening to some podcasts to get a feel for what's out there (I'm a big fan of "Stuff You Should Know"), then get recording! There will be technical issues to deal with but none of these will be hard to overcome. YouTube videos will help you work it out. Also, this excellent blog post provides a step-by-step guide: buzzsprout.com/blog/how-to-start-a-podcast

Politics. If you have political ambitions, university is the place to start. You'll find an array of opportunities to get involved in politics, such as joining campaign groups. Students' Unions are always looking for students to fill key positions too. The nature of university means that Students' Unions are revolving doors - every year, students leave and new students arrive. You should also join a political party and look into the opportunities the National Union of Students (nus.org.uk) offers. Contact your local MP too and ask about work experience opportunities. Also, there's a government website outlining other opportunities (gov.uk/government/get-involved).

Vlogging. Creating a video blog is one way to document your life or interests. Or maybe you just want to make people laugh or get lots of hits. But this isn't just a hobby.

There are some vloggers making a decent income from this (and a small minority who are killing it). Before you start, think about how vlogging could add to your life (and what you are going to say). Then have a look at your favourite vloggers (and the ones with the most followers). Record a few test videos and show them to your friends for feedback. Then choose your platform (e.g. YouTube or TikTok). Great videos will be shared, but you'll need to get the word out too.

Clubs and societies. As mentioned before, if a certain club or society doesn't exist, you can set one up. In fact, you can also set up a rival club or society, especially if what's already there isn't, for example, aligned to your beliefs. To do so, firstly you will need to contact the Students' Union, who will arrange for you to speak to the right person. Expect to have to bid for funding. This could take the form of a written proposal or a presentation (or both). If you are successful, you can expect to receive support in the form of funding, access to university facilities, advice and publicity opportunities.

Influencing. The rise of social media was swiftly followed by the rise of the influencers. In simple terms, influencers are people who have built a reputation for their knowledge and expertise on a specific topic. Of course, many of them have no formal qualifications in that area (which is always a concern, especially if they're healthcare influencers). Nonetheless, influencers can be a cause for good, and many make money by promoting goods and services to their followers. Influencing is a numbers game: the more followers you have, the more companies will be willing to pay you.

Other things you can do at university to enhance your CV (and/or your life):

1. Learn a new language. There are countless websites offering free language courses (for example, Babbel - uk.babbel.com).
2. Learn to touch type. This will also speed up your coursework. Typing Club (typingclub.com) is one of the many options available.
3. Study free online courses on platforms such as Future Learn (futurelearn.com).
4. Watch documentaries – many of which are free online (watchdocumentaries.com is great).
5. Learn how to play Chess, Go, Backgammon etc.
6. Learn how to code for free with Code Academy (codecademy.com).
7. Listen to podcasts.
8. Learn a new word every day: subscribe to receive a new word every day here: merriam-webster.com/word-of-the-day.
9. Watch TED talks: ted.com/talks.
10. Learn how to buy and sell shares: virtualtrader.co.uk
11. Learn how to draw or paint.
12. Learn digital skills for free with Google Digital Garage (learndigital.withgoogle.com/digitalgarage).
13. Meta Blueprint (formally known as Facebook Blueprint) offer essential courses for anyone interested in digital marketing: facebook.com/business/learn

Cold hard cash

Although student life is rich in many ways, money tends not to be one of them. Being canny with your money can make a huge difference to your university experience. Money management is also a vital life skill, so hopefully this chapter will help you onto the road of financial security. I've split this section into 10 parts, as there's a lot to cover:

1. Learn how money works
2. Household bills
3. Other bills
4. Travel costs
5. Holiday travel
6. Bank accounts
7. Budgeting
8. Tax on earnings
9. If you get into financial trouble
10. Money saving tips

Learn how money works

Unfortunately the teaching of financial literacy skills at school is still poor. Moreover, as most school children aren't financially independent, the lessons on offer are inevitably theoretical. So, it really is up to you to learn how money works. If you don't understand taxation, the impact of interest rates and inflation, cumulative interest, ISAs etc. it's likely this will cost you at least tens of thousands of pounds during the course of your lifetime. There are lots of free guides available on websites such as moneyhelper.org.uk and moneysavingexpert.com which will teach you the basics. If you're looking elsewhere online for advice, please carefully check the source - the internet is awash with so-called experts (usually driving around in rented supercars) telling you how to get rich quickly. Be sceptical - many are scammers who charge for financial courses which are, in almost all cases, smoke and mirrors.

Top tip: The Martin Lewis Podcast is excellent.

Household bills

If you are privately renting, you will need to pay (or legally avoid paying) the following:

- **Council tax**. As a student, you do not need to pay council tax (assuming it's just students living in the property). However, this "discount" is not automatically applied. To make sure you don't get landed with this unwelcome bill, you need to register here: gov.uk/apply-for-council-tax-discount
- **Gas and electricity**. As a private renter you have the right to change your gas and electricity supplier. And changing suppliers could potentially save you hundreds of pounds a year. To find the best deals check out MoneySavingExpert's Cheap Energy Club. Note: At the time of writing, household energy costs are rising fast and good deals are non-existent. Let's hope this changes in 2023.
- **Water bills.** Historically, these have always been paid by landlords. However, this is changing, so check before you sign the tenancy agreement. If you are liable, water companies are regional monopolies, so you can't switch suppliers. But, if you're on a water meter, try to reduce water consumption by, for example:
    - o Taking shorter showers - try the five-minute shower challenge.
    - o Turning the tap off. People who leave the tap on when brushing their teeth waste six litres of water a minute. Ouch!
    - o Getting your landlord to fix that dripping tap. Or waste roughly 5,500 litres of water a year.

- o   You can also save on water and energy by not overfilling your kettle - only boil the amount you're going to use.
- o   Always fill up your washing machine and dishwasher before you turn them on. Wash your clothes on a lower temperature setting too.
- **Broadband**. As most bills have continued to rise, the cost of broadband has continued to fall - that's the impact of a truly competitive market. Depending on where you live, you may be able to get broadband without having a landline. For the best deals, head to one of the price-comparison websites, such as uSwitch. As an aside, some broadband providers offer bundled packages, such as mobile SIM only and broadband, which are often very competitive. **Top tip:** Get high-speed broadband if you're living in a house share - it's likely that you'll be operating numerous wifi-enabled devices concurrently.
- **5G**. With the roll out of 5G combined with the falling price of data, you may find you don't need broadband - hotspotting is increasingly becoming a viable option.
- **TV licence**. You will need a TV licence if you watch television (any channel, live or catch-up) on a desktop computer, console or TV/digital box. However, if your parents have a TV licence, you don't need one if, according to TV Licensing, "you only use a device that's powered solely by its own internal batteries, you will be covered by your parents' TV Licence. However, you must not install the device (e.g. plug it into the mains) when using it to receive TV." So, it's possible to avoid paying for a TV licence, but you need to be careful - if you get caught watching television illegally you can be fined up to £1,000 (plus legal costs). If, however, you do

buy a TV licence, you can claim back calendar months (e.g. July, August) when you're not living at the property. Go to the TV Licensing website for more details (tvlicensing.co.uk).

Other bills

- **Mobile phones**. Whilst not strictly speaking a bill, mobile phones do now fall under the need category. Almost always, it's cheaper to buy a SIM-free phone and then find the best call/text/data package. However, if you need a new phone, this could mean a significant up-front cost. On the upside, some new phones are available on interest-free credit - so hunt these deals out. For the best contract and SIM-only packages, head to a price comparison website such as Money Supermarket (moneysupermarket.com).
- **Top tip**: Don't pay for data you don't use. If you're coming to the end of a contract, check to see how much data you've used each month. Make sure your new contract reflects that. Loyalty rarely pays, so ditch your current provider if there's a better deal out there. Porting your number is now pretty straightforward.
- **Top tip**: Despite all the network providers stating they had no intention of reintroducing roaming charges in the European Union post Brexit, all have - which is a disgrace. Most include some data as part of their packages - at the time of writing, O2 is the best out there, offering 25GB of free roaming data in the EU per month.
- **Airtime Rewards**. Sign up to Airtime Rewards (which works on most major networks). Link your account to your mobile number, register all your credit/debit cards, and every time you spend at certain retailers, you will get cashback which will reduce your mobile bill.

- **Insurance**. Research has shown that one in five students is a victim of theft while at university. As such, it may be worth considering buying contents insurance to insure your possessions against, for example, being stolen. Endsleigh (endsleigh.co.uk) is one company that specialises in student insurance, but don't assume they will be the cheapest. Again, head to the price comparison websites to find the best deals. Check the small print too: insurers are notoriously nitpicky when it comes to paying claims. It's important that your possessions are insured outside the home too, for example. Note: Your landlord is responsible for building insurance (to protect against any significant damage to the property), so make sure you only buy contents cover.

Top tip: If you find yourself living in a house share, set up a joint bank account, into which everyone contributes enough to cover the bills and household essentials, such as toilet paper. This will mitigate possible future arguments (and, let's face it, money disputes cause a lot of disagreements).

Travel costs

Travelling to and from university and home can be costly. Your commute between your accommodation and your lectures can be expensive too. Here are some ideas to reduce your travel costs:

- **Cycling**. In terms of local travel, having a bike will almost always save you time and money. If you don't own a bicycle, you may be able to buy a cheap second-hand one on eBay (or similar). Alternatively, post a Wanted advert on Freecycle (freecycle.org) - if you're lucky, someone might give you a bike.

- **Top tip:** Buy a good quality D lock. Getting your bike stolen isn't an option. Also, lots of cities and towns (including Brighton, Leicester, Liverpool, London, Northampton, Oxford, Reading and Southport) have public bicycle hire schemes. If you don't want the hassle of maintaining your own bike, these are a great option. Most allow you pretty much unlimited travel for a fixed annual fee, provided you adhere to certain terms and conditions.
- **Cadge a lift.** If you happen to befriend someone who owns a car, good news! They may well be heading to the same places as you. Don't forget to offer to contribute towards petrol costs, or your lifts will soon dry up. If you need to get home at the end of term, you can advertise around university to see if anyone is heading in the same direction. You never know, you might make a friend for life (you'll have two things in common already). If you're feeling brave, hitch hiking is also an option – although, I would always suggest travelling in pairs.
- **Coach travel**. This is a much cheaper option compared to train travel and offers more destinations too. To find the cheapest tickets, go to CheckMyBus (checkmybus.co.uk). Megabus is cheap as well (uk.megabus.com). In terms of student discounts, full-time students are able to buy a National Express Young Persons Coachcard. For £12.50 a year you get a third off their standard fares.
- **Train travel.** This is often expensive, but it's a lovely way to travel, especially if it's a long journey. There are ways to reduce the cost of train travel too:
  - o   Get a 16-25 Railcard. It costs just £30 and it'll save you 1/3 on rail fares throughout Great Britain for a whole year.

- o Book 12 weeks in advance. The cheapest tickets (often the ones that are advertised) usually sell out fast, so try to buy your ticket as soon as the tickets for that day are available (which is usually 12 weeks beforehand).
- o Split your ticket. For example, you want to travel from London Euston to Manchester Piccadilly. But it's cheaper to buy a ticket from London Euston to Birmingham New Street, and then another ticket from Birmingham New Street to Manchester Piccadilly. Looks like an annoying job, right? Wrong! Various apps, such as thetrainline will do the hard work for you. Note: you never have to get off the train - you just show the inspector the relevant ticket depending on where you are on the journey.
- o Advance tickets are cheaper than rocking up on the day of travel, so always book online beforehand. Many, but not all, train operators allow travellers to book advance tickets on the day of travel, so you should be able to get cheaper tickets even if you book online when you're travelling to the station.

Holiday travel

As a university student you'll have lots of long holidays, so now is the time to slake your wanderlust. If you book off peak (in terms of dates, days and times of day) and early, you'll be able to travel even on the tightest of budgets. For flights, Skyskanner is hard to beat (skyscanner.net). You can even select "Everywhere" as a destination and set a budget. Who knows where this will take you? Of all the budget airlines, Ryanair is the cheapest (ryanair.com).

Top tip: If you're looking for flights online, search in an incognito window. This will avoid being tracked via cookies, which means the prices are less likely to rise when you're next online.

Note: Airports are ridiculously expensive for snacks and drinks, as they have a captive audience - so, make sandwiches in advance and pack your bag full of snacks.

In terms of accommodation, staying in youth hostels or even sofa surfing (couchsurfing.com) will cost less than almost any other option. But, if you're travelling in a group, don't write off AirBnB (airbnb.co.uk) for larger shared accommodation options. Also, consider booking overnight tickets (be it plane, train or coach) as that will sort out your accommodation for the night too!

If you are completely skint, you can see the world by going on virtual tours. Google the place you want to go (plus "virtual tour") to see what's available.

Bank accounts

All banks are keen to grab their share of the student banking market. They're playing the long game of course: graduates tend to earn more than non-graduates and people are more likely to get divorced than change banks. So what do banks do to lure students to their shores? Hand out loads of freebies. So, see what's on offer, and open a few bank accounts. But do your day-to-day banking with the bank that offers the biggest 0% overdraft. Unfortunately, it will be hard to stay in the black as a student, so not paying for your overdraft is crucial - unauthorised overdrafts will cost you big bucks, typically 40% APR. If you are one of those lucky few who thinks they will stay in the black, search for the bank account that pays the best rate of interest. Google "best student bank account" to narrow down your search. In addition, app-based bank accounts, such as Starling and

Monzo, definitely offer more features, such as budgeting tools, real-time notifications of money being spent and in-app card cancellation.

Top tip: Once you graduate, ditch your student bank and find the best graduate bank account.

Budgeting

"The person who doesn't know where his next dollar is coming from, usually doesn't know where his last dollar went" - unknown.

As mentioned before, your maintenance loan is paid in three instalments over the course of the academic year. And provided you applied in plenty of time, you should be paid in September, January and April. For most students, this will be their main source of income, and they will need to make each payment last.

To help with this, you should create a budget plan. In simple terms, this should include all your income and all your outgoings on a month-by-month basis. Always budget for your needs initially - that could include rent, food and mobile phone. You will then be able to see how much you have left to spend on non-necessities.

Some tips for helping you create a great budget plan:
- Use one of the many free budget planner apps - the "Emma Budget Planner" is great.
- Work out when your bills go out. Your bank statements and past bills will help with this task.
- If you have to estimate a cost, over-estimate rather than under-estimate.
- Make a note of any cash payments - otherwise you will have no record of these.

- Revise and amend your budget plan each month. As you get a better idea of your costs, your plan should become increasingly accurate.

Top tip: As student loans are paid in three instalments, you will need to budget term-by-term. However, when you graduate, you will have to budget month-by-month. As such, some monthly budgeting when you are at university will help you acquire this crucial life skill.

Top tip: At university you will inevitably be in numerous situations where you need to split the bill. Download the Splitwise app to simplify this. It allows you to split, pay or receive payments. In addition, the app keeps a running total of what is owed. You can form different groups with various people and break up what each person owes. Debts can be paid or monies received via PayPal.

Tax on earnings

There's a persistent myth that students don't have to pay income tax. Everyone has to pay income tax (unless you live in the Cayman Islands). But you only have to pay it if you earn above a certain amount of money. At the time of writing that amount is £12,570. So, provided you earn less than that during the financial year (6 April to 5 April), you don't have to pay any income tax. However, some students find themselves with an "emergency tax code" and will see that tax has been deducted from their wages. This will be because the HMRC (His Majesty's Revenue and Customs) doesn't have enough details to be able to assess your tax code. For example, you haven't given your employer your P45 or you don't have a P45. But, fear not, this money should come back via your new tax code. You'll need to inform your employer and they should be able to sort this out. They may ask you to complete a starter checklist if you don't have a P45. If, after a few months, you're still paying tax, you should contact the HMRC.

In terms of National Insurance, you only have to pay this if you earn more than £242 a week. After that, it's 12% of everything you earn over that amount.

Note: Taxation rates change annually. Always check online for the latest figures.

If you get into financial trouble

In this situation, the first thing you must do is accept that there's a problem. Ignoring financial struggles won't make them go away. And there are people there to help:

- If you are in debt, the debt charity Step Change (stepchange.org) offers expert advice (online or over the phone) to help you deal with your debts. They will work with you to create bespoke and practical debt solutions.
- Another organisation to contact is the National Association of Student Money Advisers (nasma.org.uk) who have advisers located in many universities.
- Citizens Advice (citizensadvice.org.uk) is another organisation that can help. In fact, Citizens Advice can offer advice and guidance across a wide range of issues, from legal issues to housing issues.
- Most universities have hardship funds to support undergraduate and postgraduate students who fall into financial difficulties. Check on your university's website for details.

Money saving tips

There are countless micro money saving ideas that will help your finances stretch further. This list is not comprehensive, nor is it in any particular order. But, hopefully, you'll pick up a few good ideas:

- Student nights are cheaper. Lots of bars and nightclubs will have dedicated student nights (often mid-week), which will be much cheaper in terms of drinks and entrance fees.
- Two-for-one cinema. Meerkat Movies is available to customers of comparethemarket.com, offering 2-for-1 Odeon cinema tickets every Tuesday or Wednesday when you buy a qualifying product. Find the cheapest product they sell (which could be as little as a few pounds) to get a whole year's worth of cheap cinema tickets.
- When you go to the cinema, don't buy drinks or snacks there (where they are very expensive). Instead, fill your bag with cheap goodies beforehand from, for example, Iceland. Some cinemas don't seem to like this, but it's not against the law, so who cares? If you don't like the thought of being too conspicuous, start noshing when the lights go down.
- Cut the cost of haircuts. There are countless hairdressing colleges offering free or heavily discounted haircuts. Many hairdressers also have certain days when you can get a free haircut, if you're happy for a trainee to cut your hair. Look for the "models wanted" sign. Or, if you're feeling even braver, invest in some hairdressing scissors (and/or clippers) and get trimming. Student discounts may be available at regular hairdressers and barbers too.
- Check your mobile phone bill every month. Make sure you're not being charged for extras. If you are, see if you can eradicate these costs. For example, some networks charge for sharing contact details via text (which you can do for free on WhatsApp).
- Food. A big chunk of your budget will be spent on food. So, how do you eat like a king on a student allowance? Here are some ideas:

o Learn to cook. Not only will this save you loads
   of money, you should end up healthier too.
   Most ready meals and takeaways are packed
   with salt or sugar (or both). Recipes are free
   online and YouTube has loads of how-to-cook
   videos. Cooking with your housemates can be
   great fun too - especially if you're all
   reasonably incompetent.
o Shop towards the end of the day, when the
   yellow money-off stickers start to appear.
   Remember, "best before" dates are different
   from "use by" dates. The former is not a
   deadline to consume, and some supermarkets
   have now scrapped "best before" dates
   completely to avoid waste.
o Markets are usually cheaper. I'm not talking
   about posh farmers' markets, rather the
   traditional fruit and veg markets. Head along at
   the end of the day with a rucksack to pick up
   some great bargains.
o Buy One, Get One Free (BOGOF) offers are
   there to be exploited. Make sure you mainly
   buy non-perishables (such as toothpaste,
   shampoo, shower gel etc.). Buying too many
   perishable goods can lead to waste. Team up
   with a friend if you need to, to take advantage
   of this type of offer.
o Aldi and Lidl are the UK's two main discount
   supermarkets. The range of products is smaller
   compared with the larger supermarkets (such
   as Sainsbury's or Tesco), but they are much
   cheaper. The quality is getting better all the
   time too.
o Take out food is cheaper in supermarkets. So,
   that's where you should buy pizzas, chicken
   tikka masala etc.

- o Wholesalers, such as Booker, are where to head to buy pretty much anything in bulk. The downside is that you need to get a wholesale card. So, if you know anyone with their own business, ask them to apply for one. Or you could try blagging it - fill out the online application form and hope for the best.
- o Don't go food shopping when you're hungry. You'll end up buying more than you need. Mind you, if you go after a hearty lunch, you won't buy enough. Somewhere in the middle is best.
- o Switch to own-brand products. It's said that people buy products for rational reasons and brands for emotional reasons. Now is the time to be shrewd. For example, Tesco's cheapest can of baked beans currently sells for 27p; their most expensive (Heinz) sells for £1.40. That's more than five times the price!
- Don't pay for music. The basic version of Spotify is free. So is the basic version of YouTube. Amazon Prime offers members loads of free music too.
- Get a Totum card (totum.com). This doubles up as an official proof of age ID. Totum is "powered" by the National Union of Students (their word, not mine). This card will give you access to over 300 student discounts. The cheapest Totum card, Totum Digital, is actually free - the most expensive, Totum Pro, will cost you £34.99 for three years' membership. The free digital-only card offers, as you would expect, fewer benefits. The paid-for cards also come with a free Tastecard, which gives members 2-for-1 dining/50% off at 1,000s of restaurants across the UK. At the time of writing, there's a 90 day free Tastecard trial on offer - what's not to like?

- Price check anything you're planning on buying costing more than £5 online. Sort by price 'low to high' to find the best prices.
- Second hand doesn't mean second best. Second hand clothes, for example, sell for a fraction of their initial price and many have hardly been worn. You can pick up some great bargains in charity shops and vintage stores. It's better for the planet too.
- Depop (depop.com) is a great app that allows people to buy/sell clothes. You can also find heavily discounted clothes and shoes on Schuh (schuh.co.uk/imperfects) and Off Cuts Shoes (offcutsshoes.co.uk).
- Toiletries can be expensive, so work out what you really need. Soap is often much cheaper than shower gel, for example, and also uses less packaging. Discount supermarkets, pound shops or Savers often have toiletries at much lower prices than places like Boots or Superdrug. If you need to go to Boots, use your Advantage Card every time, then use the points to buy your Christmas presents!
- If you want to save a stack on perfume, Google "smell alike perfumes" to find cheap perfumes at, for example, Lidl, that smell just like designer scents.
- Student discounts are offered by loads of companies, but some are not advertised overtly. So, always ask if they are available. Note: Apple offers student discounts on almost all of their products and Amazon Prime Student is just £4.49 a month (and the first six months is free - sign up for the free trial period). If you're in a houseshare, you just need one Amazon Prime Student account - provided the member is willing to order items on behalf of their housemates.
- Groupon (groupon.co.uk/programs/myunidays) has amazing deals for students too, such as 2-for-1 meals and cinema tickets.

- Haggle. Although not embedded in UK culture, haggling is a great way to get a discount. Smaller shops, in particular, are often willing to sell products for less than the label price.
- The best things in life are free. And that includes going for a walk, outdoor gyms and many museums and galleries.
- Charge your gadgets on campus.
- Don't buy all the books on your reading list, as they will all be available in the library (and many will be available online). Only buy the ones that are essential - and buy these second hand or as ebooks (which are normally cheaper). Negotiate with students in the years above you to get their hand-me-downs. Similarly, try selling books in your second and third years that you no longer need.
- If you're studying a course that requires a high-quality laptop/Mac (design, architecture etc.) wait for Black Friday in November. This will give you time to talk to peers and tutors and establish the best equipment to buy. Then, hopefully, you'll be able to secure an amazing discount come Black Friday.
- Packed lunches and thermos flasks. Bringing your own food and drinks to university will save you hundreds of pounds over the course of your studies.
- Eating out. See who offers student discounts and look online for vouchers. Also, if you're planning on drinking alcohol, see if there are any BYOB (Bring Your Own Bottle) establishments nearby. Buying booze from supermarkets will cost a fraction of the amount restaurants charge. If you can't find any BYOB restaurants, head out pre-loaded (but not too pre-loaded).
- Voucher codes online. There are various websites that publish reams of voucher codes (Google "voucher codes" to find them). Don't go there as a first port of

call. Rather, if you are shopping online and during the checkout process there's a voucher code box, see if you can find one. That way you'll get a discount on something you planned to purchase anyway.

- Get a Pret Subscription - If you frequent coffee shops, it might be worth getting a Pret Subscription, which allows you to get five Barista-made drinks (coffees, teas, hot chocolates, smoothies etc.) a day for £25 a month. There's no tie-in period, so you can cancel at any time. You can also pause the offer for a month - which might be useful between terms. (If you canned this offer, and bought five drinks every day for a month, you would save over £400 that month alone.)
- Collect reward points with loyalty cards, such as Nectar and Tesco Clubcard.
- Don't pay for international phone calls - use WhatsApp, Skype or Facetime instead.
- G Suite from Google. I'm a sucker for all things Google and with good reason. The Google versions of Microsoft's Office programmes are far better and are all free. Replace PowerPoint with Slides, Word with Docs, and Excel with Sheets. Google Drive gives you 15GB of free storage. All of these programmes integrate with Gmail, Google calendar etc. and are available as apps too.

Final thoughts: Before buying something always question yourself. Do I need it? If not, don't buy it. Also, if something breaks, see if it can be repaired before you rush out and buy a replacement. This will save you money and save on landfill.

Academic studies

Although there's lots going on at university (and you should take advantage of this as much as you can), you are there, primarily, to get a good degree. So, preparing for and keeping on top of your academic studies is super important.

Transition from school to university

Before you even arrive at university, it may be required (or at least advisable) to do some academic preparations. Make sure you read everything your university sends you. Read that article, do that problem set, answer those questions.

The key difference between school and university is that, at university, no one is going to worry if you don't do the work. There will be some key deadlines you must meet, seminars you must attend and so on. But there won't be a detention if you don't turn up for a lecture. Therefore, self-motivation is key. Here are some tips to make that happen:

- **Have a growth mindset** not a fixed mindset. A growth mindset means you believe that, through your actions and hard work, you can change and develop. You can improve at subjects you find difficult and your abilities are not set in stone, but are under your own control. A fixed mindset is just the opposite. Train yourself to develop a growth mindset - this will help in your studies, especially if you find them challenging, and will set you up well for the world of work post-university.
- **Focus on why you're there.** You have applied for and been accepted at university because you want to get a degree and you understand the advantages this may give you in your life ahead. Keep focussed on that big picture when you face those early

morning lectures and essay deadlines.

- **Manage your time.** Different people have different ways of doing this, so choose what works for you. But here are a few key ideas:
  - o **Make a to-do list** and keep it updated. This can be a real list with pen and paper or a digital list e.g. on one of the many to-do list apps. Having a comprehensive and ongoing list means that things do not get forgotten and you will know when deadlines are approaching. Making the list at first may seem like a big time cost (and therefore counterproductive) but it will save you so much time in the long run. Plus, you get the satisfaction of ticking things off!
  - o **Do one thing at a time.** Don't get distracted by text messages when you're in the middle of reading an article. Don't worry about essay 2, when you're doing essay 1. Work in chunks of time (say 25 minutes) and allow yourself to do other things between those chunks but not during them. Google "The Pomodoro Technique" for a time management method based on working in small chunks of time.
  - o **Beware of social media.** Social media is specifically designed to keep you addicted. You may think it's not a big deal, but it's going to seriously impact your efficiency if you keep looking at Instagram feeds. Give yourself times when you allow yourself to look at social media, and times when you don't. And turn off those notifications to avoid being tempted.
  - o **Don't do things at the last minute.** There's always going to be some variation between people: some prefer to have everything done with loads of time to spare, others can't get going until the deadline pressure is on and then

they thrive on it. Work out which you are, but always plan ahead.

o **Try to prioritise your academic studies**. University is awash with opportunities - sporting, social, societies, entrepreneurship, campaigning, events, politics etc. that you should embrace, especially if you want to be amazing. Nonetheless, it has to be business before pleasure. Get your academic work done early and efficiently to give yourself time for extracurricular activities.

Lectures. You may or may not need or want to attend a lot of lectures. It very much depends on your particular course and university, the structure of the course, and the quality of the lectures themselves. If lectures are a required part of your course, you'll have to go. Make the most of them by taking careful notes, and keeping those notes in an organised way as you proceed through the course. It's a lot easier to do five minutes of document sorting (electronic or paper) at the end of each day, than a whole day's worth in a panic in the approach to exams. By the way, you won't remember what went on in a lecture, even a very short time afterwards, even if you think you will! Always take notes (even if the lecturer is providing notes too).If it's an optional lecture course, attend the first one. You'll get the measure of whether it will be helpful, how to access resources, and you might find out some interesting things. Whichever lectures you decide to attend, stick to it. It's frustrating to have half a set of notes and no way of obtaining the rest.

Another thing to think about is to team up with a friend - each of you attends one lecture course and gives the notes and resources to the other one. Or investigate whether your department makes lectures available online.

(But, beware: many lecturers intentionally keep some resources only for those who attend in person.)

Seminars and tutorials. Again, depending on your particular course and university, these may be frequent or few and far between. If they're compulsory, go! Chances are that the person running them may have an impact on the grade you get. And don't be afraid to ask questions and get involved - you will learn a lot more that way. Check whether you need to do anything to prepare, and meet the deadlines. In some universities, and for some subjects, tutorials may be in very small groups or even one-to-one. You're going to feel pretty silly if you arrive, haven't prepared and need to explain yourself.

Remote learning. Although the amount of remote learning has reduced considerably since Covid-19, there is still some university learning taking place online. There are some benefits, as you don't have to drag yourself to the lecture hall. But there are temptations too - it's easy to slip into bad habits such as multitasking and becoming a passive learner. You have to be disciplined - and things like getting showered and dressed before an online lecture will help you get into a better mindset to fully engage. Also, make sure you are as equipped as you would be if you were attending face-to-face lectures and tutorials.

The library. There will be a library or libraries where you can loan out books or use books for studying inside the library. Use these resources. Not only does it save you money buying expensive textbooks, but it will also focus your mind if you work in the library from time to time.

Also, the librarians tend to know a lot about useful books, and sometimes there will be a librarian allocated to your particular subject. Many electronic versions of books are available too, so you may be able to borrow from the library without going there in person. The library will also give you access to academic websites, publications and journals. There will almost certainly be a long list of available websites and you should work out which are relevant for your subject. You will probably need to use your university login to access these.

Working with others
There are a number of great ways to team up with others on your course or in your halls of residence:
- Team up on lecture attendance as mentioned before.
- Check in and communicate about deadlines. It's always good to know that someone is also keeping track of dates, so you have a double check.
- Proof read or check each other's work. It often helps to have a fresh pair of eyes on an essay, or someone's input on a problem set.
- Ask those in the years above. Don't just stick with your own year group. After all, there are probably people in the year above who did the same task last year and can help you out.
- Set up a study group. This is especially helpful with brainstorming for ideas or if you know you struggle with self motivation.
- Offer your help to others. After all, what goes around, comes around.

Top tip: There will always be people who talk a good talk but don't necessarily have anything to back it up. There will always be those who say they did no work, but come out with the best mark in the class. Don't believe them!

This could be particularly relevant to you if you're female. There are lots of statistics to show that female students tend to speak up less than their male classmates. But there is nothing to suggest that male students come out with overall better grades in the end.

Academic writing

Typically, the style of writing required will be particular to your subject and the published literature in that field. Your supervisor or department may also have some particular requirements. Take note of these and follow them. Beyond that, here are some good general tips:

- **Quality over quantity.** Your supervisor won't be impressed by long waffly sentences and big words, unless they mean something. Write in a pithy way and get to the point. Remember - your supervisor has read lots of work before and will easily spot if you are trying to dress up your lack of knowledge in long sentences.

- **Practise your speed reading.** You may need to refer to lots of articles and books and the more you practise, the faster your reading will become. You will also get better at searching a text for the information you need. Also, practise taking notes from multiple sources and develop your own systems for keeping those notes in some sort of order.

- **Reference the sources you use.** The particular books, papers and articles you refer to must be referenced. Your supervisor will advise you on how to do this, as there are lots of formats out there. But do it, and do it well. You can even get an add-on that links directly to Google Scholar. (More on Google Scholar and other apps for studying later.)

- **Plagiarism.** The first rule is to remember that your supervisor has read a lot more on the subject than you have. If you are reading a paper, chances are they have come across it before or at least know the author. You must not plagiarise. Firstly, it will be spotted - much more easily than you think. Secondly, it could get you in serious trouble if you are presenting others' work as your own.
- **Dissertations.** At some point in your degree course, you will almost certainly need to write a long essay or piece of writing known as a dissertation. This will probably be 10,000-15,000 words for an undergraduate degree. The same points apply here, with added emphasis on planning ahead and keeping your work organised.
- **Save your work!** Sounds pretty obvious, but there are a remarkable number of students who lose their essay in the run up to the deadline, because they dropped their computer or similar stories. Even better, use a cloud-based system, so you don't have to worry about pressing Save.

Science subjects
If you are studying a science, maths or another related degree, you may never need to write an essay, but you may find these tips helpful instead:
- **Lab work.** You may have full days in the lab. These can be really fun and a great way of obtaining course credit in some cases. But they can also be tiring and can take up a lot of time. Don't plan on spending a full day in the lab, followed by an evening of last minute studying. Be prepared for them by turning up on time and doing any necessary preparation. Depending on your course, you may also want to wear clothes you don't care about too much.

- **Problem sets.** You may have problem sets instead of essays. And these may require the lecture or seminar notes before you can even think about doing them. Bear that in mind when deciding which lectures to attend. And, remember that you may have to do quite a lot of reading before you can tackle the work itself.
- **Be prepared to do a lot of work by hand.** At the time of writing, there is no software that can replace doing mathematical work by hand (rather than typing). So, chances are, you may need to use a lot more paper - and do a lot less typing - than arts students. Prepare for this, by having plenty of paper and decent pens and pencils, especially if you've got a deadline coming up. Alternatively, you may want to write mathematical work electronically using a stylus or similar. There's lots of great tech out there and it's getting better all the time. Beware though - if you need to write exams with an ink pen on paper, this may be a shock if you're not used to it.

Revision and exams

There are lots of books and websites out there focussed solely on revision techniques and preparation for exams. But here are a few key tips:
- **Plan ahead.** You may not think you need to start revision yet, but if you work out what exactly needs to be done and how long you have to do it, this will be reassuring. Remember - there may be things you need to do before you can even start revising, such as obtaining those notes from your friend, downloading course notes, or obtaining that book from eBay.

- **Be active not passive.** Passive techniques such as reading notes and books tend to be pretty ineffective. Chances are your mind will wander or you'll doze off because it's not particularly riveting. Much better to take active steps such as writing out revision notes, doing practice problems, making essay plans and so on. At the very least, if you have to simply read something, do it while walking around your room so you don't lose concentration.
- **Use standard techniques.** There are lots of ideas out there, but approaches such as mind maps, flash cards, study groups with friends are all great.
- **Avoid stress.** Exams can be stressful, but keep them in perspective. Final exams (known as just finals) are not the be all and end all and will, in time, feel considerably less significant (just like GCSEs probably do already). Remember - not everyone will have the same stress points as you, but they won't have the same strong points as you either. Play to your strengths: if you know you don't sleep well the night before an exam, prepare for it. Don't plan to do lots the next evening, and don't worry when you're wide awake. If you know you have a tendency to run late, set out your exam stuff the night before - including the clothes you're going to wear. If you know exams stress you out, protect your mental health by using the techniques detailed in the "Health & Wellbeing" chapter of this book. And keep remembering that all you can do is your best.
- And finally, **don't do post mortems.** If you come out of an exam and feel it went well, don't tell everyone around you. They don't want to hear it. Similarly, if you feel it went badly, don't listen to others boasting about their success. Get yourself a cup of tea, pull your socks up and focus on the next one.

Apps for studying
There are thousands of different apps that you might find helpful in your studies. Compare with your classmates to find the best ones. But here are a few to get you started:

- PDF scanner – Turn your mobile into a scanner with one of the many PDF-scanner apps. I use Genius Scan and it's great!
- Google Translate - Google's app supports over 100 languages. Plus the app's accuracy is improving all the time.
- Google Docs - There are lots of reasons this is a great app, but the photo to text feature is really neat. Take a photo of some text, and it will convert it into editable text. (Google Docs also has a super referencing tool.) Plus it can read to you! And you can store all your documents in Google Drive.
- Grammarly - More than 20 million people use Grammarly every day. It's an AI-powered app that helps you write mistake-free text.
- Google Scholar - search for articles (and US case law) on your topic of interest - great for finding your source material.
- Referencing apps and add ons such as EasyBib and RefME. Apps like these make referencing and bibliography creation easy. Universities are nitpickers when it comes to referencing, and poor referencing will lose you marks.
- Apps for creating study and revision resources such as flash cards and mind maps. Examples include StudyBlue, GoConqr and SimpleMind.
- Note-taking apps such as OneNote and Evernote allow you to stay organised with all your notes in one place.

- "Disability" apps - There are lots of apps, such as voice-to-text apps, designed to help students with, for example, dyslexia. So, if you do have a "disability", Google these apps.

Top tip: Learn how to use "Advanced search" - google.co.uk/advanced_search. This allows you to search by file type (e.g. PDF or PowerPoint), country, language, date etc. Whittling down your search results to the best ones will save you loads of time and improve your academic work. To learn how, watch YouTube tutorials.

Different types of courses
Most university courses will follow a straightforward three or four year programme, all in the same location. But, there are some things you might need to consider if your course has a different structure, for example:
- **Sandwich courses.** A sandwich course involves spending some time in industry during your degree programme. Usually this is for a year after the second year at university, but it could comprise smaller placements throughout the university course. The key advantage of a sandwich course is that you'll gain relevant work experience and make industry contacts. And this should help you secure a job when you graduate. If you are on a sandwich course, make sure you are fully prepared for any academic work you need to do at the same time. Ensure you manage your time carefully and have access to all the resources you need.
- **Study abroad courses.** A number of courses, typically those involving languages, linguistics or literature, involve a year overseas, usually after the second year at university. Indeed, over 20,000 students study/work abroad every year. This option will not be open to all students, however. So, speak to your tutor in advance. If it is an option, they will point you in the right direction.

Some reasons to study abroad:
- It will be an experience you'll never forget. You'll experience new cultures and you may learn a new language. And, if you choose wisely, you may spend a year in the sun.
- It's great for your CV and, when it comes to seeking graduate employment, it will make you stand out from other candidates. We live in a global economy, so cultural awareness is a valued commodity.

Getting a job
This section has been split into five parts:
- Finding a part-time job while studying
- Work experience/internships
- Sandwich year employment
- Graduate jobs
- Entrepreneurship

Finding a part-time job. Supplementing your Maintenance Loan with income from paid employment could hugely improve your quality of life. And all employment looks good on your CV. Working is also another great way to meet new people. Don't worry if you lack experience. Employers will be prepared to offer training if you arrive with a positive can-do attitude (and a big smile on your face). Indeed, The Confederation of British Industry (CBI) has identified possessing a positive, can-do attitude as a key employability skill, alongside things such as team-working, problem solving and self-management, none of which are linked to having relevant work experience. That's not to say work experience isn't important - it is. But, it's less so when you're looking for part-time work. Lots of student jobs are advertised on the appropriately-named Student Job website (studentjob.co.uk). But, don't rely on the internet. Lots of jobs aren't advertised and walking the streets is a great way to find these hidden jobs. Print a pile of CVs and then ask local bars, restaurants, nightclubs, coffee shops etc. if they're looking for staff.
Remember, students give a big boost to local economies and seasonal job opportunities rise and fall in line with university term times. Plus the range of jobs available to students is broader than most people think. Aside from the more common student jobs, there are quirky jobs too, such as becoming a film extra or signing up for police line-ups. Joblift has kindly compiled a list of 40 different part-time

student jobs:
joblift.co.uk/career-insider/40-part-time-student-job-ideas
Competition for student jobs can be fierce though.
Consider this example: the working aged population of
Leicester is approximately 237,000 and, of those, 41,000
are students - that's 17%. Granted, some students in
Leicester will be living at home, but that's still a huge surge
in numbers.

Top tip: While everyone else is partying during freshers'
week, spend a bit of time investigating job opportunities. At
this point lots of businesses will be hiring and not many
new students will be applying for jobs.

Work experience/internships. Once you enter the
graduate job market you will be in competition with,
obviously, other graduates. So, you will have to work hard
to get noticed. One way to get noticed is to have relevant
work experience on your CV. Indeed, a recent survey
published on the UCAS website showed that two thirds of
employers look for graduates with relevant work
experience. Finding opportunities that will give you this
experience will not be easy and, for many students, it may
not be affordable. Companies have been fairly criticised for
years for nepotism and for expecting students to work for
free. Wealthier students tend to have the contacts and the
money to deal with these issues. If that's you, use your
contacts. Who wouldn't do the same in your position? If
that's not you, here are some tips:
- The best internships/work experience opportunities
  arc snapped up fast, so start your search early. If
  you're looking for a summer holiday internship, that
  means early in that calendar year.
- Have a great CV. There are free CV templates and
  examples online, and your university should have a
  careers department that can help.

- Talking of which, ask your careers department and your subject department to help. They should have good contacts. Also, Google "work experience and internships" - you will find lots of relevant websites.
- Create a great LinkedIn account and start networking with people working in your field of interest.
- If you have been working part-time, ask your employer to write you a written reference (and keep a digital copy of all your references).
- Fill out lots of applications and send your CV to lots of people. Finding good work experience is often a numbers game. It's a bit like trying to get your first book published: expect a lot of failure on the road to success. (Kathryn Stockett's "*The Help*" was rejected 60 times before being published, selling over seven million copies and being made into a multi-award-winning film.) Don't take rejections personally; they are part of life. Instead, dust yourself down and get back on the bike.
- Expect to have to complete online tests. These are often very similar, and practice makes perfect. So, make sure you complete a fair few of these before applying for your ideal internships.

Note: In your first year, most internships take place during the spring holiday. In your second year, internships are usually run during the summer holiday. If you land a spring internship and your employer likes you, they will, hopefully, fast track you onto their summer internship. Spring internships tend to have early deadlines - that could mean October of the year before.

Top tip: Sign up to Bright Network. They host loads of events that enable you to boost your CV and network (brightnetwork.co.uk).

Sandwich year employment. This only applies to students on four-year sandwich courses. In terms of finding this type of employment, the same rules apply as finding work experience or an internship. The big difference is the role of your faculty. As a placement year is built into the course, they will have relationships with various relevant employers. The important thing to remember is this: they will only recommend the best students for the good jobs. If your attendance at lectures and tutorials is poor, you'll fall down the pecking order. You have been warned. (From the university's point of view, they will want to protect and nurture these employer contacts; as such, they will not want to burden companies with unreliable students.)

Graduate jobs. So, what is a graduate job? It's either one that relates directly to the subject you studied or one that offers a graduate training scheme.

Most students graduating with vocational degrees (such as dentistry or archaeology) will look for work in those sectors. Other graduates probably shouldn't limit their job hunting to jobs that relate to their degrees; the majority of graduates don't end up working in their field of study: psychology graduates get jobs in marketing; media graduates get jobs in financial services; arts graduates end up in sales. So, unless you're completely sure of your chosen career path, don't limit yourself. Getting a degree shows you're smart and motivated, and that's what employers want. Indeed, many tech companies and other innovative businesses are far more interested in your ability to learn than what you already know.

There are approximately 1.8 million undergraduate students studying at UK universities. And roughly 400,000 new graduates enter the job market each year. Of those, 28% will have first class degrees (up from 7% 25 years ago). That means employers are often spoilt for choice. It's not all doom and gloom though: most years, more than 90% of graduates have gained employment (or have continued studying) within six months of leaving university.

Many employers will prioritise students with top degrees from good universities (e.g. one of the 24 Russell Group universities). Graduates in shortage subjects will definitely have an advantage too. Nonetheless everyone needs to try to stand out from the crowd (and 400,000 graduates is definitely a crowd). Having a great CV and written references will help. Here are some tips for getting noticed (or not rejected):

- Have a great CV. Include anything out of the ordinary (such as the kind of things included in the "How to be amazing" chapter). Also, find out what businesses want and add that to your CV. (As mentioned before, the Confederation of British Industry (CBI) regularly publishes a list of skills employers desire, such as team-working, problem solving and digital skills.) Remember, people are busy: keep your CV pithy. If someone is faced with a pile of CVs, they are likely to skim read them anyway. **Top tip:** If you're posting your CV or handing it out, get it printed on good quality, watermarked paper - it will look much better.
- Regularly update and improve your LinkedIn account and start networking during your final year (if not before). Some companies will accept your LinkedIn URL as your job application, covering letter and CV rolled into one.
- Write speculative letters. If you are confident you know the sector in which you'd like to be employed don't wait for the jobs to be advertised. Instead, you can write speculative letters to prospective employers. Outline why you want to work for that organisation and the skills, experience and

enthusiasm you will bring. Include your CV and written references (if you have them). Ideally post your speculative letters and follow up with an email/phone call a few days later. **Top tip:** Always write to a named employee (ideally a decision maker or someone working in the Human Resources department). You should be able to figure out the right person with a little online research.

- Covering letters. These allow you to expand on your CV and make your application more applicable to the job for which you're applying. Covering letters should outline how you think you can benefit the company you're applying to - for example: "I have read that you are currently recruiting new staff. As such, I thought I would write to you to outline how I think I can benefit your organisation. I possess many skills I hope you will value. I am reliable, hardworking, and a quick learner. Moreover, I am a self-starter who gets on well with people - I'm definitely a team player. I am also polite and helpful. My teachers and friends would describe me as dependable, punctual and trustworthy. As such, I believe I possess the attributes you require to become a successful and productive employee. But I know I need training too - and I would embrace any training opportunities available - there's a lot for me to learn!"
- Social media accounts. Change all your privacy settings, so only your friends can find you. Also, delete any controversial posts/photos. Or take the nuclear approach and delete some or all of your social media accounts.
- Google your name (especially if it's an uncommon name). If anything bad comes up, you can evoke the "right to be forgotten". Google this for details.
- Get a sensible email address.

Milkrounds. This is the term used to describe events that allow companies to promote their companies and recruit students directly. Traditionally the process involved recruiters attending university careers fairs. In recent years, this has largely shifted online (milkround.com). During the autumn term of your final year, you should start using this website to look for suitable opportunities.

Other notable job websites:
- Indeed.com - This website lists tens of thousands of jobs. As well as searching for jobs, you can also upload your CV and research companies.
- Jobs-graduate.co.uk - As its name suggests, this website offers a huge range of different graduate jobs and opportunities.
- Totaljobs.com - Another website that lists tens of thousands of jobs every month. It has a nifty alert tool too, which will notify you if a relevant job appears.
- Google "Graduate jobs" to find even more job websites.

Interviews - top tips:
- Double check the time, date and address of the interview. And find out the name of the person who will be interviewing you.
- Research the role and the employer before the interview. Often prospective employees will be asked what they know about the organisation. Drawing a blank is not an option.
- Research the person who is interviewing you too. It might be that you have some common ground, which could help swing the interview.
- Research interview hints and tips online - there are some great videos on YouTube.

- Rehearse. Role-play is pretty cringe worthy. However, it does work. Practise introducing yourself and answering some typical questions, such as, "Why should we employ you?"
- Bring three copies of your CV, some paper and two pens. You may be asked to complete some written tasks. Bring copies of your references too.
- Dress to impress. This may include getting a haircut.
- Arrive early. There's no such thing as too early. If you have 30 minutes to kill, walk around the block a few times. Five minutes before your interview is due to start, introduce yourself to the receptionist (and turn your mobile phone off). Be super polite and charming - receptionists are gatekeepers and often hold the keys to the kingdom.
- When the person interviewing you arrives, introduce yourself, shake hands, make eye contact and say their name back to them. Thereafter, you're in the lap of the gods. However, if you have done your homework, the interview should go well. If it doesn't, that's okay. Think carefully about what went wrong and learn from your mistakes.
- Body language is important. Sit up straight, don't fold your arms, try to avoid annoying habits (such as tapping your foot) etc.
- Make sure you ask questions at the end of the interview - for example, "What training will I receive?" or "What is staff turnover like?" The point of the questions you ask is for you to appear keen - you may not be that interested in the answers!

- Most importantly, change your mindset. President John F. Kennedy's inauguration speech included the line "Ask not what your country can do for you – ask what you can do for your country". What *can* you offer your prospective employee? That's what they want to hear. Even if it's just "blood, toil, tears and sweat" (to quote Winston Churchill).

Entrepreneurship - It's reckoned that each year 4,000 graduate start-ups are created. So, perhaps it's better to create your own employment. After all, the self-employed are happier, according to research conducted by the University of Sheffield. There's more about starting your own business in the Entrepreneurship section of the "How to be amazing" chapter.

The things that you can't control:
- If **the economy** is booming, most graduates will find landing a graduate job reasonably easy. However, if the economy is in a slump or recession, or we're in the midst of a global pandemic, it might be much harder. Those students who graduated in the aftermath of the global financial crisis found it very hard going, as did the "Covid-19" graduates. If you find yourself in this position, firstly, go easy on yourself. If you can't find a graduate job, it's not really your fault (blame the bankers instead). Secondly, keep on studying and acquiring new skills to add to your CV - there are lots of free courses online, for example, MOOCs (Massive Open Online Courses). Or choose a different tack, such as studying for a Masters. Accepting a non-graduate job is fine too. However, if possible, get a job in a company that has a graduate trainee scheme, as you may be able to transfer onto that scheme at a later date.

- **The rise of Artificial Intelligence (AI)**. The world is evolving fast: the spread of automation, robotics and artificial intelligence is likely to influence the working lives of all of today's university students. There are now robots undertaking kidney transplants and AI-powered programmes writing news articles.
- In November 2022 the beta version of ChatGPT launched which could accurately answer most academic questions and, more amazingly, it could write academic essays (and much more). How will this affect university study? No one knows for sure - but the wise will view this as an opportunity, rather than a threat. The same goes for the various AI drawing apps.
- No one can be certain how these developments will affect the job market either. But the pace of change will be fast. The winners in this new world are likely to be those with transferable skills, those who are flexible, and those willing to embrace change. As Bill Gates once said, "Evolve or die". Remember, many jobs that exist today didn't exist 20 years ago.

Health and wellbeing

This section covers physical, mental and sexual health, as well as some "staying safe" tips. The content is designed to stimulate thought, as opposed to provide all the answers. Not least, because no one knows all of the answers.

Physical health. Staying fit at university can be challenging. Many students are living rule-free lives for the first time. As such, it's easy to slip into a life of partying, Netflix and Deliveroo. And there's nothing wrong with that for periods of time. But you have to be careful that this doesn't become your life and you fail to achieve your goals. It's also worth noting that more than 50% of first year students put on weight (and some 25% lose weight). So weight-change is a significant factor for many freshers. Some tips for keeping healthy:

- Don't smoke or vape. Almost everyone who starts to smoke regrets it. Nicotine is highly addictive and once you're hooked it's very hard to stop.
- Don't drink alcohol every night and try to avoid too much binge drinking. Drinking alcohol is a high-calorie occupation too. There are, for example, 227 calories in a pint of Stella Artois.
- Illegal drugs. These should be avoided. If you find yourself with a drug problem, seek professional help.
- Exercise every day. Even if it's just a walk to the shops.
- Join university sports clubs or go to university exercise classes.
- Try to eat lots of fresh fruit and vegetables. And avoid too many takeaways and ready meals (which will be laced with sugar and salt).
- Avoid soft drinks - they are full of sugar and have no nutritional benefit. Diet (zero-calorie) drinks don't help either - a study in the journal Obesity that followed 3,700 people for eight years showed that

those who drank low-calorie drinks put on the most weight. There are conflicting arguments as to why, but one theory is that when we put something sweet into our mouth, our receptors tell the body that food is on the way. But with zero-calorie alternatives that same message is sent, but no food arrives. The argument is that the link between sweetness and calories has been broken. Drink water - it's much cheaper too.

- Do the washing up. Kitchens are germ magnets and you're far more likely to get ill if you let things fester. Some other kitchen hygiene tips:
    o Never wash raw chicken (to avoid food poisoning from campylobacter bacteria).
    o Do not refreeze anything.
    o Don't cook anything that's not fully defrosted.
    o Wash the tea towels frequently.
    o Wash your hands regularly too and try to catch your coughs and sneezes - it's good to protect other people too.
    o Keep cooked and uncooked food separately in the fridge.
    o Cans are not suitable for storing food once they've been opened as the metal of the can may transfer to the can's contents (according to the NHS).
    o Use different chopping boards for raw and ready-to-eat foods.
    o Store raw meat and fish in a sealed container on the bottom shelf of the fridge.
    o If you're barbecuing meat, wait until the BBQ has cooled down a little and slowly cook the meat (turning it often). Check it has been cooked all the way through before serving. And avoid cross contamination between cooked and raw meat.

Mental health. According to Mind (the mental health charity) approximately 1 in 4 people in the UK will experience a mental health problem each year. First year students can find adjusting to university life hard, and some will suffer from mental health issues, such as anxiety and depression. There will also be other pressure points such as assignment deadlines and exams. Universities have been pretty quick to recognise this as a problem and will be able to offer help, support and guidance. But there are things you can do too:

- Stay fit. Your physical health is closely linked to your mental health. Excessive drinking, drug taking, poor diet and smoking have all been linked to mental health issues.
- Go outside when the sun shines (or when it rains). Fresh air and sunshine have been shown to make people happier.
- Don't resort to alcohol or other drugs if you're feeling down. They will make you feel worse.
- Live in the moment. Enjoy each interaction and each new experience. Consider downloading one of the mindfulness apps such as Headspace.
- Routine is good. Try to get up and go to bed at similar times each day. And get at least eight hours of sleep every night.
- Don't try to change what you can't change. Focus on the things you are in control of - the "uncontrollables" are just that. So try not to think about them (or worry about them).
- It's good to talk. If you are struggling, talk to a trusted friend. Or, if you are very worried about your state of mind, seek professional help (for example, from a GP).

- There is also lots of help online, for example, Mind (mind.org.uk), Student Minds (studentminds.org.uk) and The Samaritans (samaritans.org).

Sexual health. Sexually Transmitted Infections (STIs) affect young people more than any other age group. For example, 15 to 24 year olds account for more than 50% of all diagnoses of chlamydia and gonorrhoea. In the words of Public Health England, "Young people are putting themselves and their partners at risk of getting an STI." So, protect yourself and others by always having protected sex. That might mean buying condoms for the first time. Many find this embarrassing - if that's you, buy them online. Once you have a supply of condoms, keep them in your wallet or purse at all times. And never have unprotected sex. You can find lots of useful help and advice here: nhs.uk/live-well/sexual-health/

Staying safe. Being a victim of a violent crime is less likely than the tabloids would have you believe. Nonetheless, you can take some sensible precautions that will help you stay safe:
- Don't leave your drink unattended or accept drinks from strangers. "Date rape" drugs are easy to slip into drinks. If you need to go to the toilet, ask your friends to keep an eye on your drink.
- If possible, don't walk alone anywhere after the hours of darkness. Some halls of residence create a list of students who are willing to act as chaperones. If your hall doesn't, it's an easy thing to set up.
- If you are walking home alone at night, avoid unlit streets, parks and alleyways. Also, remove your headphones and don't talk on your mobile. You need to be aware of your surroundings and possible dangers.

- Always use licensed taxis and, even then, it's better to share a taxi with a friend (and it works out cheaper).
- Don't assume that, because it's a student night, everyone around you is trustworthy. Sadly, not all students are perfect human beings, and you still need to stay alert and take precautions to keep yourself safe.
- Help others. If you see someone in trouble on a night out, make sure they get home safely.
- Don't open your front door to anyone you don't know, unless the door chain is in place. If a work person needs access to your property, ask them for their ID before you let them in.

Dating and relationships

Research has shown that one in five students meet their life partner at university. And that's heart-warming. However, some students find themselves in messy relationships. Here are some university dating and relationship golden rules:

- Don't date your flatmate. If you split up it's not just you that suffers; it won't be much fun for your other flatmates.
- Not everyone wants to be in a serious relationship. And that might include you. Establish the parameters fast, so you know where you stand.
- Take things slowly. Changing your social media status to "in a relationship" after one date will terrify certain people.
- Do free things together - walks in the park, sunset cycles etc. - money pressures are one of the biggest causes of arguments between couples. And most students don't have much spare cash.
- Consider using dating apps. Yes, you will already be surrounded by suitable suitors. Dating apps, however, allow you to date outside your friendship groups. And that has to be a good thing.
- If someone breaks your heart, try to move on fast. Chances are you'll barely remember their name in a few years' time. Plus, never has the phrase "there are plenty more fish in the sea" been truer.
- If you have a boyfriend/girlfriend back at home (or at another university) be realistic about how often you see them. If you hook up every weekend you will miss out on university life. That's not to say you shouldn't talk every day - there's nothing wrong with that.

Top tip: Fortune favours the brave. If you find someone attractive, talk to them. Do this as often as you can. This will probably be the only time in your life when you will be surrounded by young, often hot, people - enjoy!

Help! I'm not loving university
Unfortunately, some students have a rough time settling into university life, often through no fault of their own.

Why students drop out of university. The biggest factors are money troubles and not choosing the right course or university. And, whilst it's not possible to eradicate these issues, students can work to minimise them. If you have not yet applied to university, here are some interesting facts:
- In the first year, approximately 6% of students drop out.
- The drop-out rate of some universities is three times the national average.
- The drop-out rate also varies wildly by course. Computer Science is almost 10% whereas Medicine is less than 2%.
- Students who go to a university that's made them an unconditional offer are also far more likely to drop out. This is thought to be because some universities are desperate to recruit students and, as a result, reduce their entry requirements. This, in turn, leads to unsuitable students enrolling at that university.

So, do your research. There is data available from every university and every course in the country. Choose the universities and courses with the lowest drop-out rates. They must be low for a reason. Think twice before accepting an unconditional offer - in life we sometimes treasure the things we have worked the hardest for. (As an aside, depressingly, the least well off students are far more likely to drop out too.)

Before you quit. If you find yourself contemplating dropping out, don't do anything rash. Consider the reason or reasons why. Write these down in one column. In the next column write some possible solutions. Consider the following:

- **Wrong course**. Universities do not want students to leave. It costs them money and damages their reputations. Most universities will try to agree to as many student course change requests as they can accommodate. Speak to a Students' Union representative for advice.
- **Wrong accommodation**. If you're living in university halls of residence, your university should be able to rehouse you. Again, speak to a Students' Union representative.
- **Failing your course**. If you're struggling to stay on top of your course requirements and deadlines, speak to one of your lecturers or supervisors. They will be best positioned to give you good advice. Again, bear in mind, universities are penalised if students drop out. Most universities will work with students to make sure this does not happen.
- **Money worries**. If you find yourself unable to pay your bills, see if you can access the university hardship fund. Also, of course, re-read the finance section in this book.
- **Relationship troubles** (romantic). These are, unfortunately, part of life. Try focussing on other areas of your life, such as your academic studies.
- **Lack of close friends**. Close friendships can take years to nurture, so there's no rush. If you're struggling to make friends, have you joined enough clubs and societies? You won't make friends sitting in your room.
- **Life issues**. You might, for example, end up ill, suffer a bereavement or struggle with mental health issues. Please never suffer in silence. Seek help from your university.

Graduation Day

If you've reached this far, you've made it - well done you! Now is the time to don the most ridiculous outfit you'll ever wear - your graduation gown and mortarboard. You may also have to endure your parents crying and other humiliating moments. But savour this day. There will be some people there you will never see again. Party hard and tell your friends how much you love them.

Useful websites

The standout student website is Save The Student (savethestudent.org). It's packed with great articles, useful links and the latest news and information. (To confirm: I am not on their payroll!) Moneysavingexpert.com is also excellent - their student finance guides are second to none. Finally, The Student Room (thestudentroom.co.uk) hosts some interesting online forums - these are great places to get answers to any questions you may have. Although, of course, it's not possible to vouch for the quality of the answers.

To conclude

University life is a bubble of unreality. There's nothing quite like it. Many graduates describe their time at university as the best days of their lives. That's how I feel too. I made some of my closest friends at university. I learned more in those three years than I had in the previous eighteen. And I laughed out loud every single day. University life is swift and fleeting. Enjoy every moment.

Please review this book!

If you've enjoyed reading this book (or you didn't, but you learned lots), please leave a five star review on Amazon or Good Reads. If you have spotted any mistakes or omissions, please email me: nedbrowne@hotmail.com so I can amend/improve future editions. Thank you!

Thank you

For support, proofreading and ideas: Vicky Bradford, Tom Browne, Alessandra Ciadamidaro, Aiman Shahzad and Bushra Khan.

Printed in Great Britain
by Amazon

34429396R00051